Not All Mermaids Have Fins

A Magical Activity Book for Little Learners

Fun with Addition, Subtraction,
Word Scramble, Tracing, Coloring,
and More!

Not All Mermaids Have Fins

Written by Luz Maria Mack
Illustrated by Katie Sarvas

Published by Luz Maria Mack
Printed in USA

MATCH IT UP

CAN YOU FIND THE PICTURE ON THE RIGHT THAT MATCHES THE ONE ON THE LEFT?

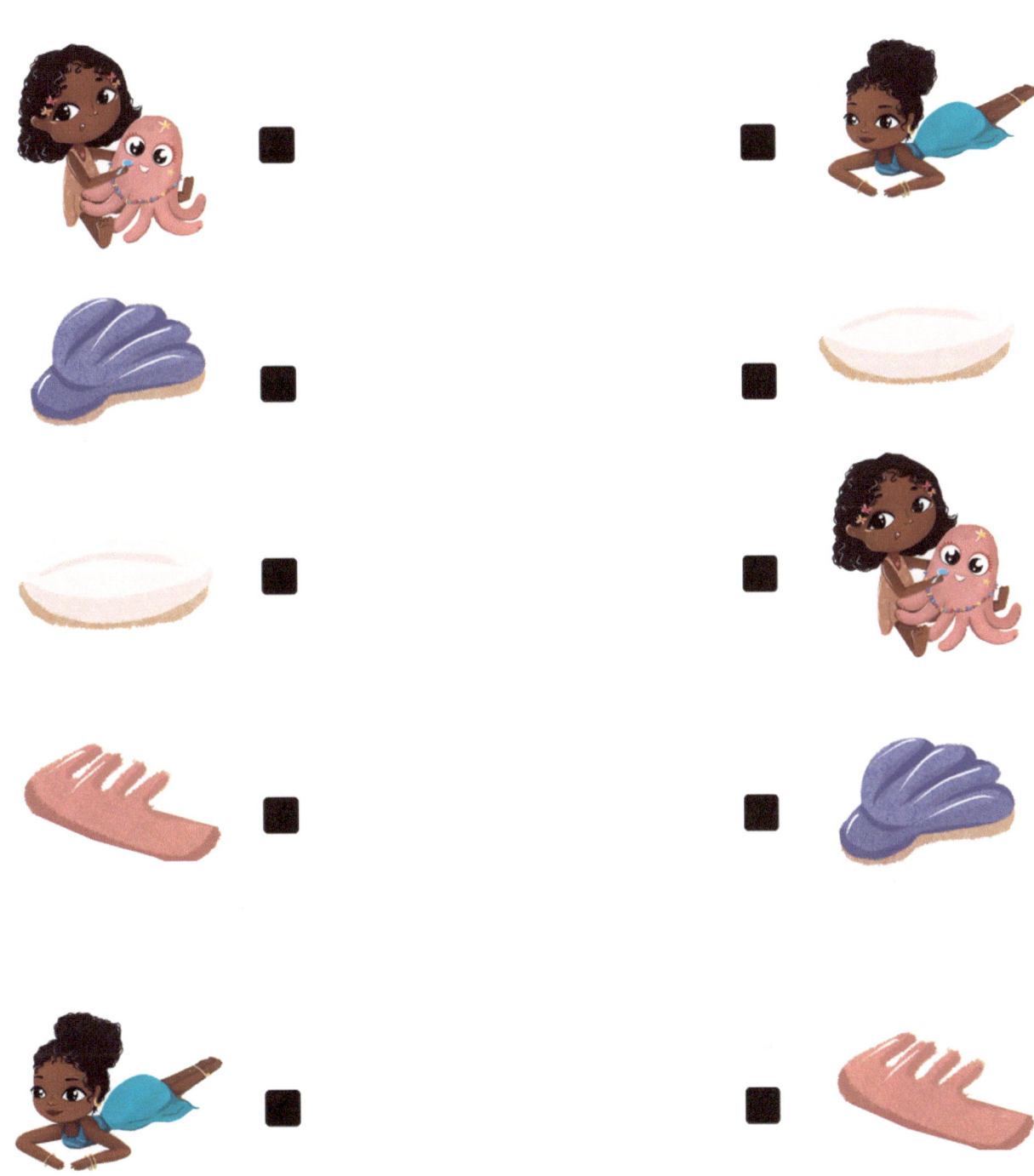

FIND AND CIRCLE

CAN YOU FIND THE RIGHT SHADOW AND CIRCLE IT?

FIND AND CIRCLE

CAN YOU FIND THE RIGHT SHADOW AND CIRCLE IT?

MATCH PICTURE

FIND THE HALF THAT COMPLETES THE PICTURE

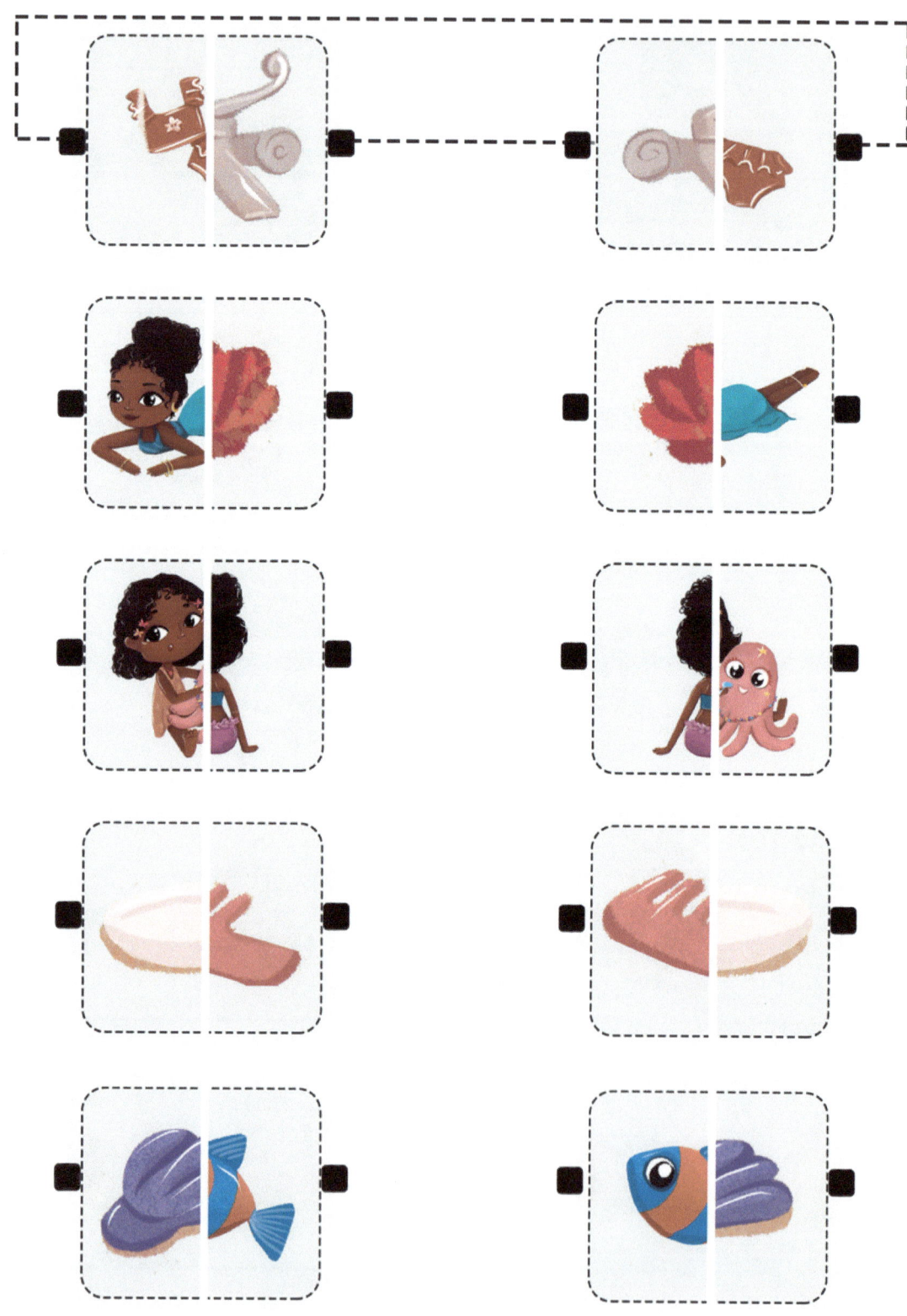

I SPY

LOOK FOR A SIMILAR PICTURE AND WRITE ITS NUMBER.

I SPY

LOOK FOR SIMILAR PICTURE AND WRITE ITS NUMBER.

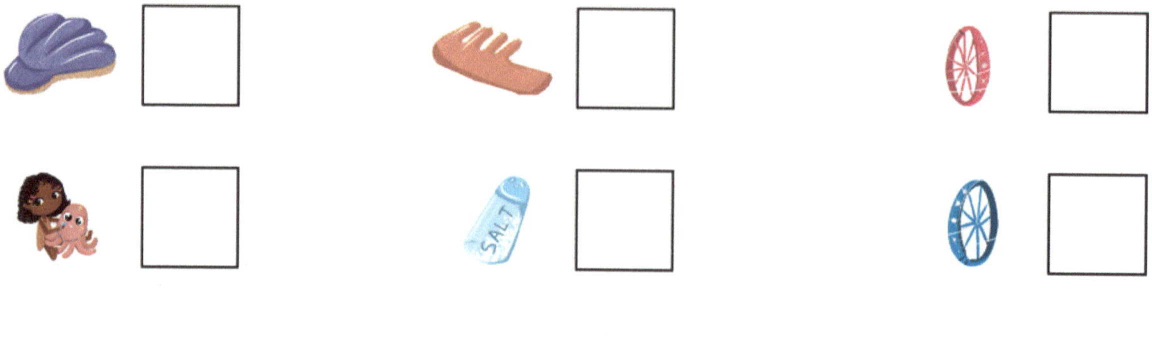

I SPY

LOOK FOR SIMILAR PICTURE AND WRITE ITS NUMBER.

ADDING PICTURES

ADD THE PICTURES TOGETHER AND WRITE THE TOTAL NUMBER.

SUBTRACTING PICTURES

COUNT HOW MANY PICTURES ARE LEFT AND WRITE THE NUMBER.

MULTIPLYING PICTURES

FIND THE TOTAL NUMBER OF PICTURES BY MULTIPLYING, THEN WRITE THE ANSWER.

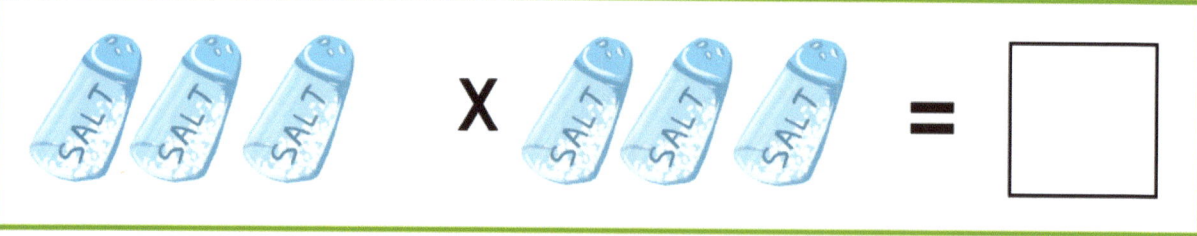

PICTURE COUNTING MATCH-UP

COUNT THE PICTURES IN EACH BOX AND CONNECT TO THE RIGHT NUMBER.

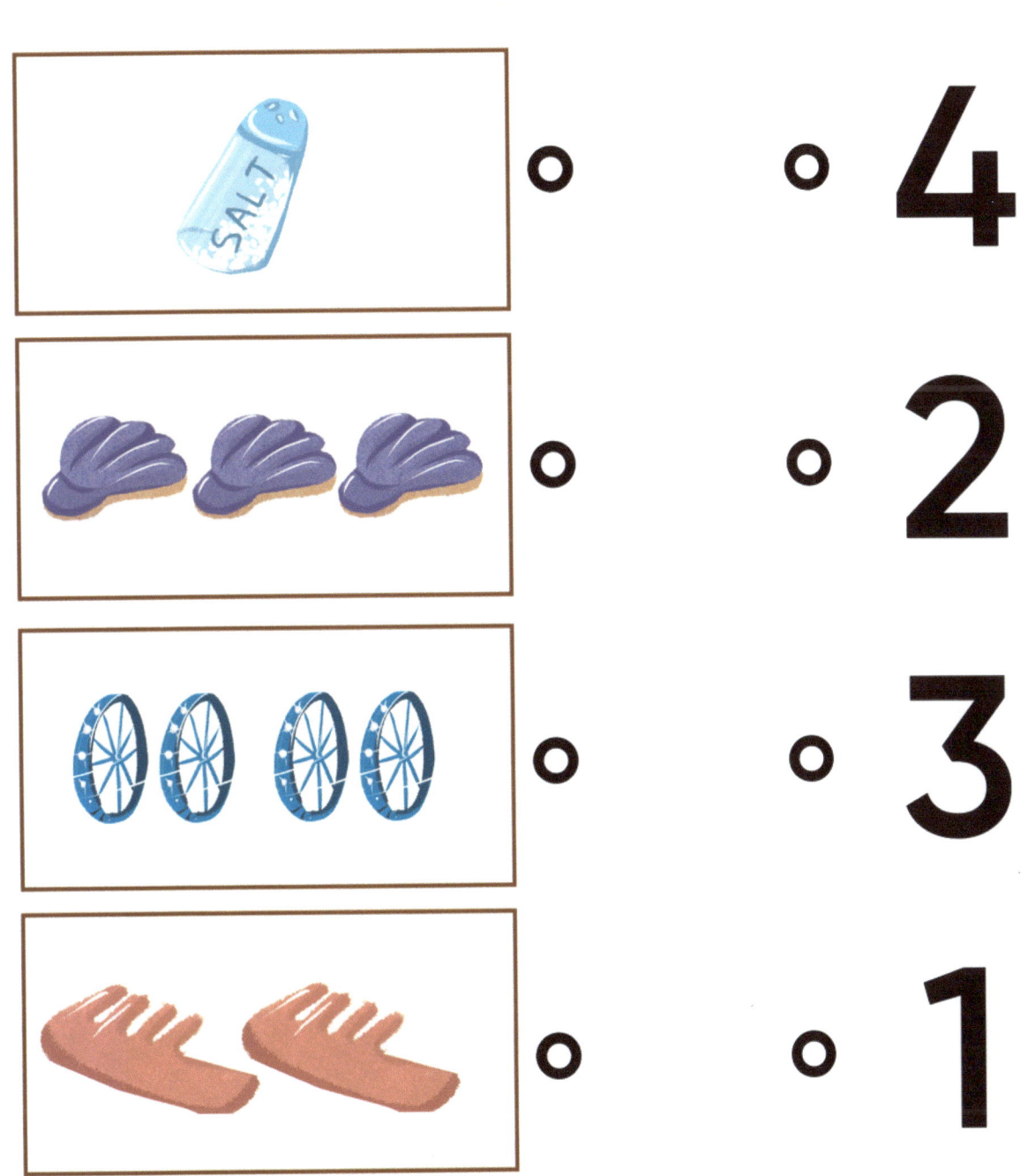

COUNT AND CHOOSE THE RIGHT NUMBER

COUNT THE PICTURES AND PICK THE RIGHT NUMMBER.

 | 6 4 5

 | 6 7 1

 | 3 5 8

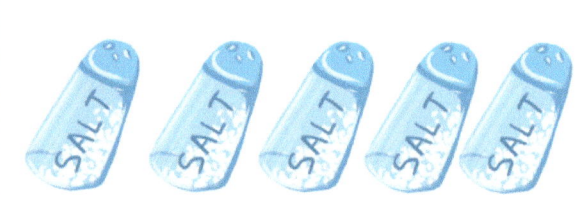 | 8 7 6

 | 10 9 8

TRACE THE LINES

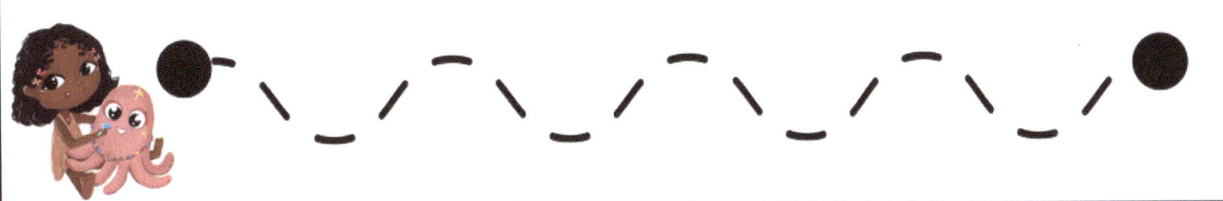

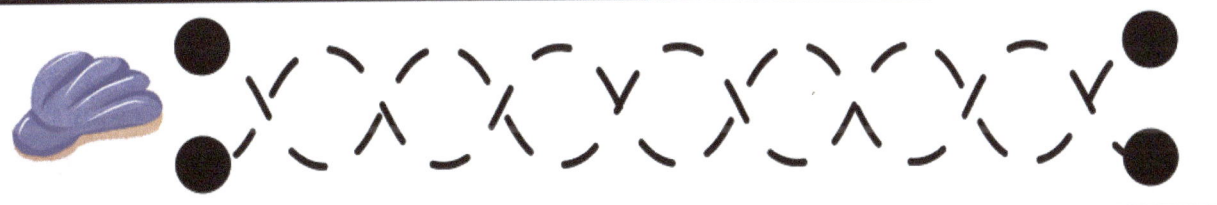

TRACE THE LINES

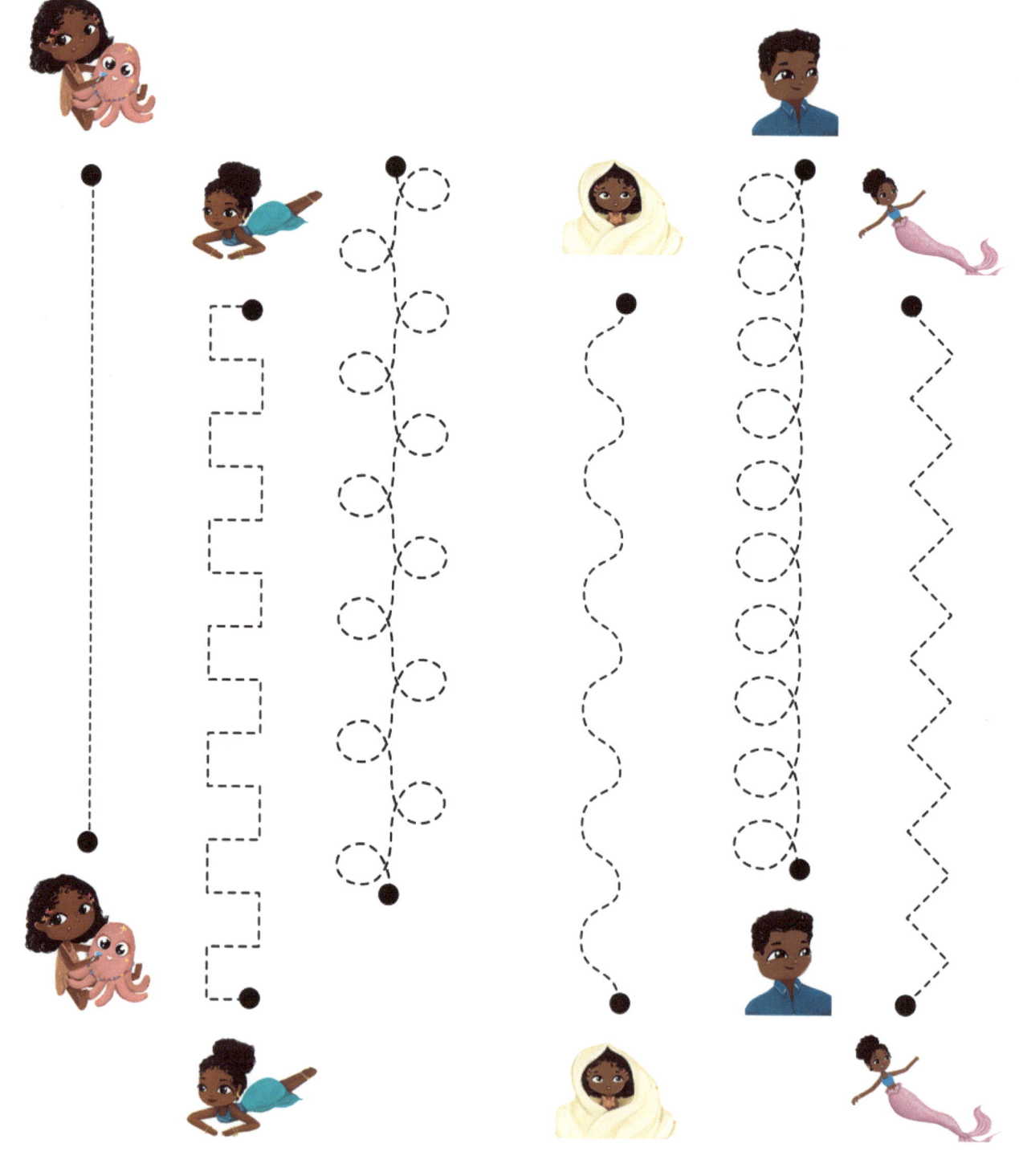

NUMBER COLOR GAME

COLOR THE PICTURE USING THE NUMBER KEY

| 1).GREEN | 2).BLACK | 3).RED |

CUT ALONG THE DOTS

FOLLOW THE DOTTED LINE WITH YOUR SCISSORS TO GET TO THE PICTURE.

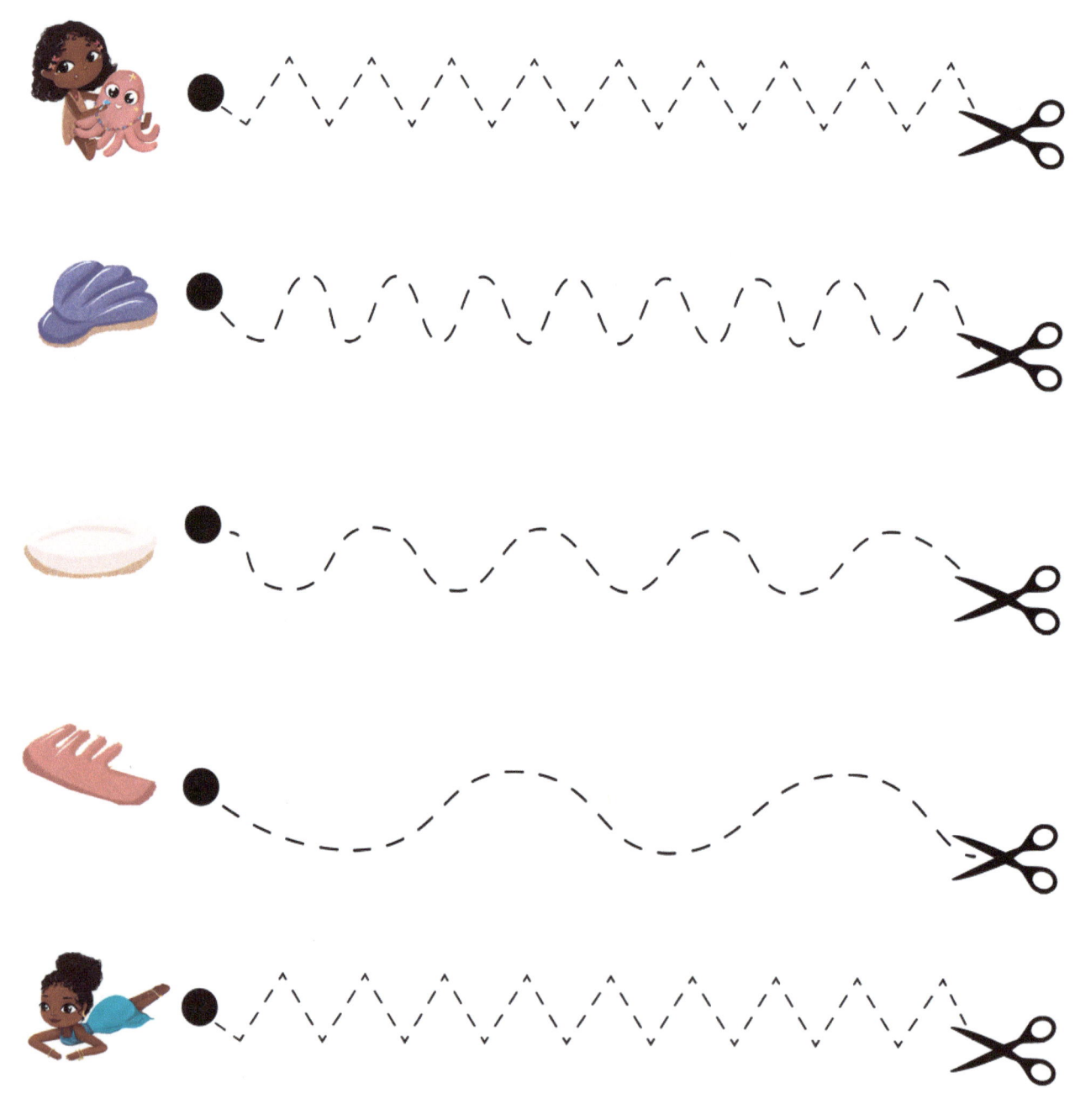

CUT ALONG THE DOTS

CUTOUT THE SALT BOTTLE AND COLOR IT.

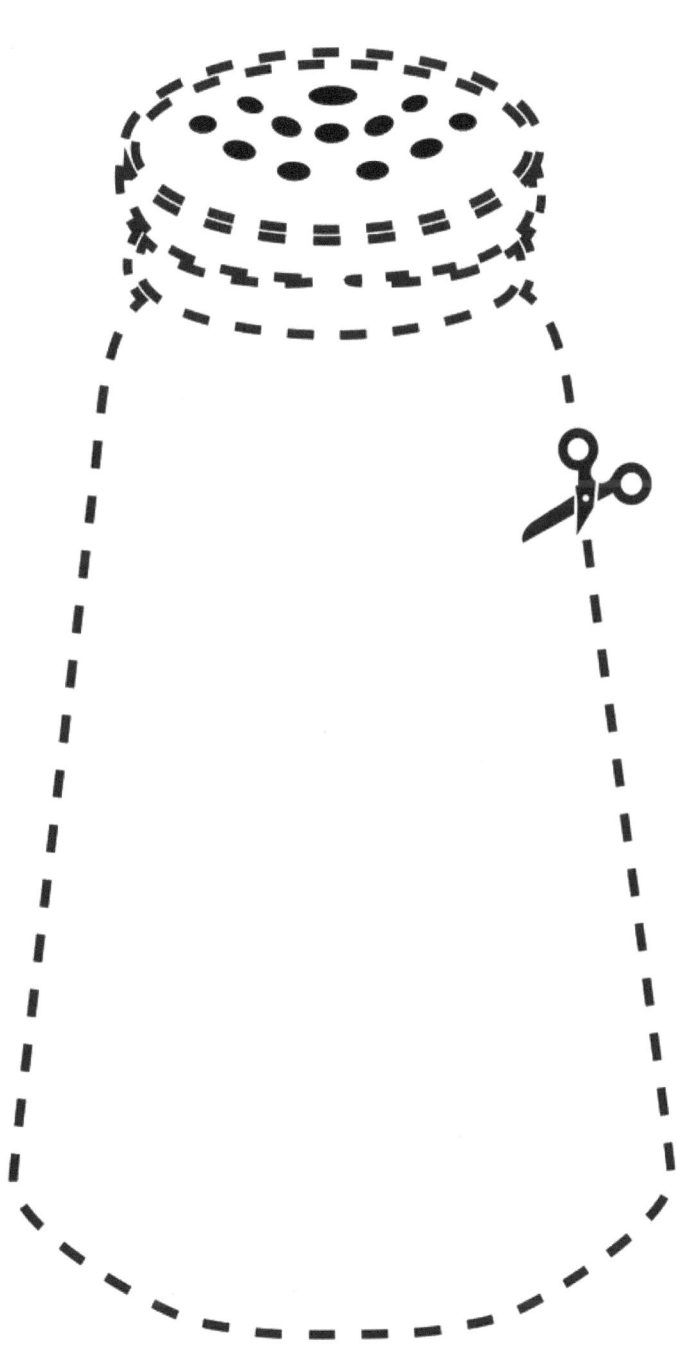

COMPLETE THE PICTURE

CUT OUT THE MISSING PIECE AND GLUE IT IN PLACE.

CIRCLE THE BIGGEST PICTURE

FIND THE BIGGEST PICTURE AND CIRCLE IT

CIRCLE THE SMALLEST PICTURE

FIND THE SMALLEST PICTURE AND CIRCLE IT

PLACE VALUE

PUT THE NUMBER IN THE CORRECT PLACE VALUE.

TENS ☐ ONES ☐

TENS ☐ ONES ☐

TENS ☐ ONES ☐

TENS ☐ ONES ☐

TENS ☐ ONES ☐

TENS ☐ ONES ☐

MAZE

HELP ANDREITA FIND THE SALT BOTTLE.

WORD SCRAMBLE

WRITE THE CORRECT WORD

1).IFNS

2).OMMYM

3).MREAMDI

4).SLAT

5).WEEHSL

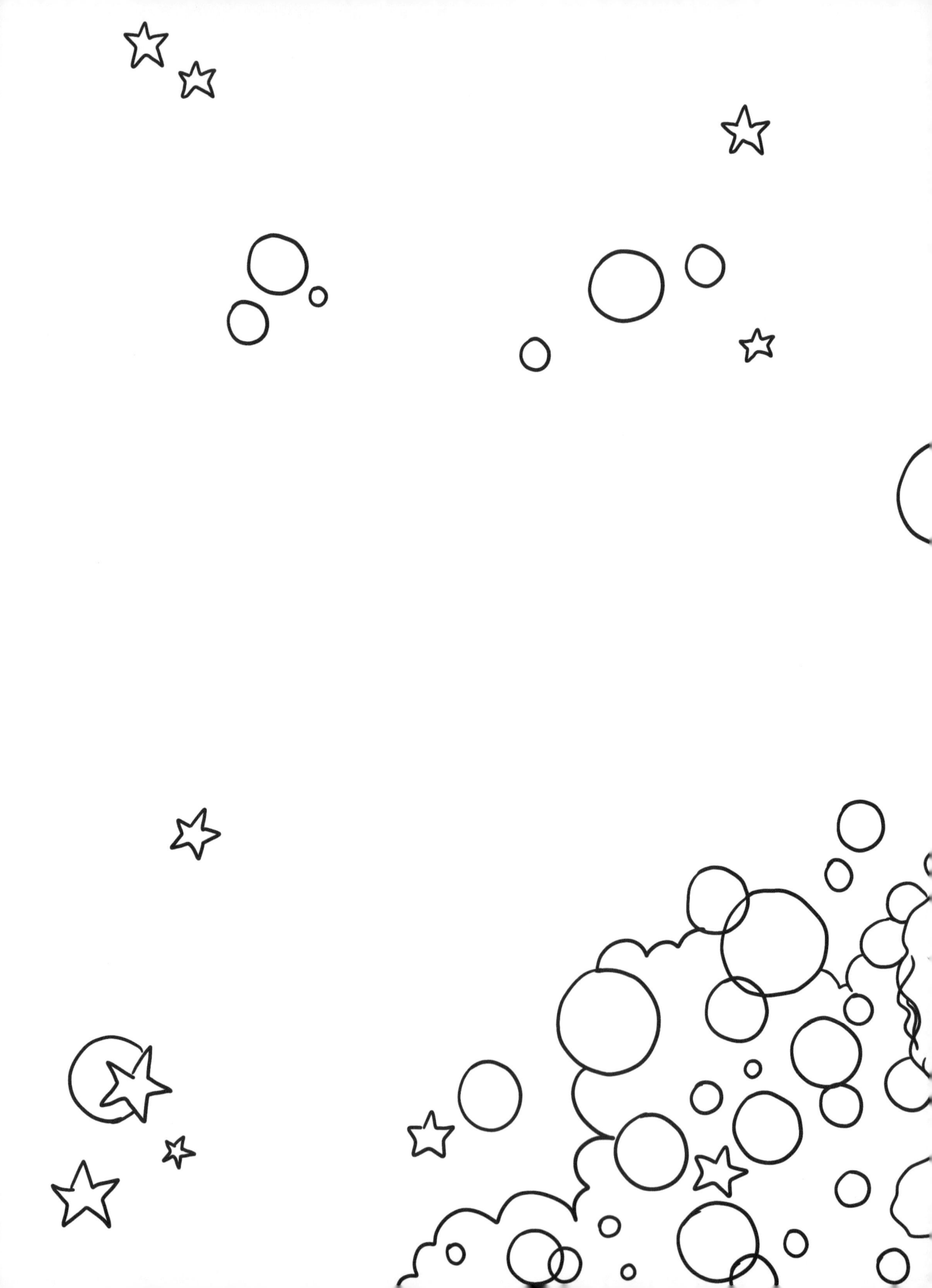